A Guide to

EGYPTIAN

Myths

By Sophie Washburne

Cavendish
Square

Published in 2025 by Cavendish Square Publishing, LLC
2544 Clinton Street Buffalo, NY 14224

Website: cavendishsq.com

This publication represents the opinions and views of the author based on their personal experience, knowledge, and research. The information in this book serves as a general guide only. The author and publisher have used their best efforts in preparing this book and disclaim liability rising directly or indirectly from the use and application of this book.

Disclaimer: Portions of this work were originally authored by Janell Broyles and published as *Egyptian Mythology* (Mythology Around the World). All new material this edition authored by Sophie Washburne.

All websites were available and accurate when this book was sent to press.

Library of Congress Cataloging-in-Publication Data

Names: Washburne, Sophie, author.
Title: A guide to Egyptian myths / Sophie Washburne.
Other titles: Global guide to mythology.
Description: Buffalo : Cavendish Square Publishing, 2024. | Series: The global guide to mythology | Includes index.
Identifiers: LCCN 2024012764 | ISBN 9781502672223 (library binding) | ISBN 9781502672216 (paperback) | ISBN 9781502672230 (ebook)
Subjects: LCSH: Mythology, Egyptian. | Egypt–Religion.
Classification: LCC BL2441.3 .W38 2024 | DDC 299/.3113–dc23/eng/20240402
LC record available at https://lccn.loc.gov/2024012764

Editor: Jennifer Lombardo
Copyeditor: Rachael Morlock
Designer: Deanna Lepovich

The photographs in this book are used by permission and through the courtesy of: Cover image AI generated by The Rosen Publishing Group using Midjourney; cover, footer, pp. 22, 30 (graphic element) berkah jaya material/Shutterstock.com; back cover, pp. 1, 3, 4, 5, 6, 7, 9, 14, 19, 24, 27, 32, 35, 40, 42, 43, 44, 45, 46, 47, 48 (graphic element) Marylia/Shutterstock.com; p. 5 Everett Collection/Shutterstock.com; p. 6 Andrea Izzotti/Shutterstock.com; p. 8 tonyzhao120/iStock Photo; p. 10 Paolo Gallo/Shutterstock.com; p. 11 TerryJLawrence/iStock Photo; p. 12 Statuette, Isis, Horus MET 04.2.443 right3 4/Wikimedia Commons; p. 13 Eleni Mac Synodinos/Shutterstock.com; p. 15 Horus and Seth crowning Ramesses III, detail of Seth/Wikimedia Commons; p. 16 Egypt dauingevekten/Wikimedia Commons; p. 18 Jakub Kyncl/Shutterstock.com; p. 20 Eric Isselee/Shutterstock.com; p. 21 Stasique/Shutterstock.com; p. 23 WH_Pics/Shutterstock.com; p. 25 James Michael Dorsey/Shutterstock.com; p. 26 AlexAnton/Shutterstock.com; p. 28 LizCoughlan/Shutterstock.com; p. 31 Vladimir Wrangel/Shutterstock.com; p. 33 Alvaro Lovazzano/Shutterstock.com; p. 34 Peter Hermes Furian/Shutterstock.com; p. 36 Vibe Images/Shutterstock.com; p. 37 Paul Vinten/Shutterstock.com; p. 38 Tasawer/Shutterstock.com; p. 39 Greece, late 5th century BC - El Hecte- Incuse Square (reverse) - 1917.982.b - Cleveland Museum of Art/Wikimedia Commons; p. 40 Karla Rutukaru/Shutterstock.com.

Some of the images in this book illustrate individuals who are models. The depictions do not imply actual situations or events.

CPSIA compliance information: Batch #CSCSQ25: For further information contact Cavendish Square Publishing LLC at 1-877-980-4450.

Printed in the United States of America

CONTENTS

Introduction   4

Chapter One: 9
An Introduction to the Gods

Chapter Two: 19
Divine Rivalry

Chapter Three: 27
Social Order

Chapter Four: 35
The Natural World

Glossary   42

Find Out More   44

Index   46

About the Author   48

INTRODUCTION

There is evidence that human beings lived and traveled through the area we now call Egypt for thousands of years before any advanced civilizations began to form. Eventually, small villages and then large cities arose on the fertile Nile River plain, and around 3000 BCE, the First Dynasty began the long age of Egyptian power.

The Nile River was relatively easy to travel, so it was not difficult for rulers to control all the people who lived up and down its length and for trade to thrive. Wild game was abundant. Wood was uncommon, but in the dry climate, mud bricks worked perfectly well for everyday housing. For grand temples and tombs, there were sandstone and limestone, although quarrying and transporting blocks of stone required enormous effort. As Egypt grew in power, traders from nearby lands brought jewels, **exotic** animals, and other luxuries to sell to wealthy nobility.

The importance of the Nile to everyday life and survival made it an equally important part of Egyptian mythology. The river symbolized life itself, and the god of the Nile had to be **appeased** in order for the Nile to flourish. However, as important as the Nile was, Egyptian mythology was ultimately centered

The discovery of King Tutankhamun's tomb in 1922 and the amazing treasures it held revived the West's interest in ancient Egypt.

around the pharaoh, or ruler. The pharaoh was seen as a god made human. It was his job to oversee all of Egypt—to ensure that the Egyptian people gave the gods the proper respect, that grain was stored up so there would be enough food in case of crop failure, that armies were raised when needed to protect the country, and that great temples and monuments were built.

Death was as important as life to the ancient Egyptians. For them, life continued after death. This belief fueled some of Egypt's greatest architecture and took up enormous amounts of its wealth and energy. Some of the earliest Egyptian settlements show evidence of the burial of the dead with the things they

Mummification played an important role in Egyptians' ideas about the afterlife. Even animals, such as this cat, were sometimes mummified.

needed or enjoyed in life, including clothes, jewelry, makeup, food, and water. As time went on, burials became more and more elaborate, especially for the wealthy. Tombs were filled with every possible tool and luxury the deceased, or dead, might need in the afterlife. There was also a rich mythology surrounding the afterlife that laid out in detail what happened to people after they died.

While this preoccupation with the afterlife can make the ancient Egyptians seem like a gloomy people, the texts and **hieroglyphs** they left behind show a people with a great capacity for pleasure, which included hunting, dancing, and eating with abandon. Perhaps the Egyptians' focus on the next world was not out of a sense of doom but out of a desire to keep the pleasures of this world going on forever, without interruption.

As time went on and the country experienced multiple invasions, Egypt's ancient language was eventually partially taken over by Greek, Latin, and finally, Arabic. Many of the great tombs were robbed of their treasures and became curiosities for Greek and Roman tourists, who went so far as to scribble their names inside the sacred resting places of pharaohs. The old gods were neglected and finally given up for the newer gods of the Greeks and Romans, and then of Christianity and Islam. During the 19th century, French soldiers even used the Great Sphinx for target practice with their rifles. We owe a great deal to the scholars, such as an ancient Greek man named Herodotus, who wrote down what they could of the rituals, myths, and customs of the Egyptians that still existed in their day.

Ancient Egypt fascinates us because it was such a rich and advanced culture, yet we still know so little about it. In addition to scholarly writings, hieroglyphs and scrolls left behind by Egyptian scribes and artists give historians a basic understanding of Egyptian religion, myths, and daily life. However, there are still many gaps in our knowledge. How many stories, songs, myths, and legends were told around the fire at night and were never written down? In addition, there are still burial places that remain unexplored or covered by the desert sand, waiting to be discovered. Perhaps there are myths and legends that remain to be found that will help us understand more about the ancient Egyptians and the ways they viewed their world.

Images of Egyptian gods can still be seen in some places in Egypt today, such as this temple in the city of Luxor.

CHAPTER ONE

An Introduction to the Gods

There are hundreds of gods and goddesses in the entire Egyptian **pantheon**. Many are local gods of the hearth and field, or different **aspects** of the same gods in different villages. The identities of the gods sometimes blurred as old gods fell out of favor and new ones arose to take their places. While it was easy for ancient Egyptians to keep track of these changing deities, or gods, it can make things difficult for modern researchers attempting to organize all the names, powers, and roles of each god and goddess.

Below is a list of some of the most important gods and goddesses, their backgrounds, and the roles they played in Egyptian society.

Ra

Ra, also called Re or Amun-Ra, was the god of the sun. Most Egyptians knew him as the main creator god as well. Ra is the oldest Egyptian god. After he was born out of an ocean of **chaos**, he created the rest of the early gods, the earth, and humanity. He could appear as the sun itself or as a man with the power of the sun. As the sun, he sailed through the sky each day in his sky boat and then through the underworld in his night

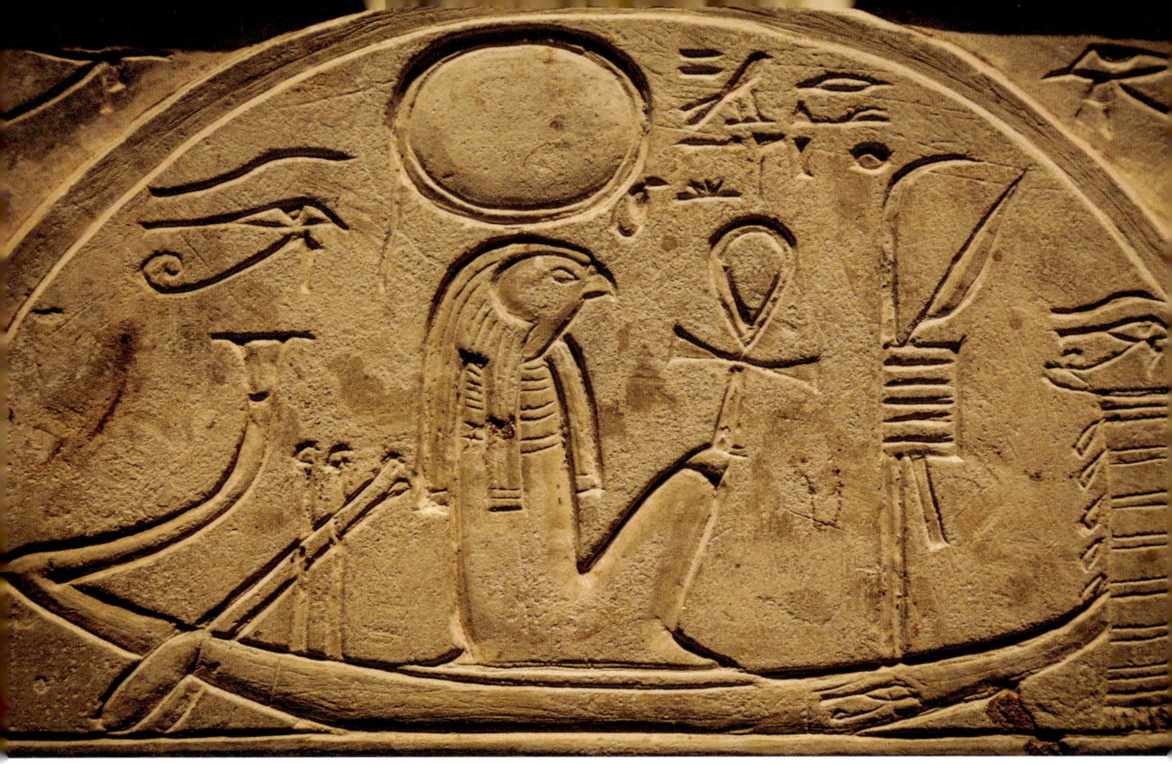

This carving shows Ra, in his aspect as Ra-Horakhty, being rowed across the sky in his golden boat. The sun above his head makes it clear that this is Ra rather than Horus.

boat. Every night in the underworld, Ra was attacked by a giant, evil snake named Apophis. The Egyptians believed that if Ra did not defeat the snake, the sun would not rise in the morning and the world would end. Ra was a symbol of divine, or godly, order and power. He kept the world in balance in all things. He also welcomed the souls of the deceased and personally took them to the underworld on his golden boat.

In later Egyptian history, Ra was merged with other gods. One of these was the falcon-headed sky god Horus, which is why Ra is sometimes drawn with a falcon's head. As one god, they were called Ra-Horakhty, and they controlled the sun and the sky. The Egyptians believed that the pharaoh was an incarnation of Horus, and his connection to Ra gave him absolute power. The god Amun, one of the most powerful in Egyptian history, came from Ra. This is why their names are often written together. Amun-Ra was Ra's aspect of order and control. In his aspect as creator, Ra's name was used almost interchangeably with the creator god Atum.

Osiris

Osiris was the god of the dead. He was the oldest child of the earth god and the sky goddess. Osiris was said to be the first pharaoh, who taught humans how to farm and gave them the laws of civilization. He was married to his sister, Isis, who was the goddess of fertility. Osiris and Isis are so closely linked that Osiris is sometimes associated with fertility as well. After his murder and resurrection, or rise from the dead, he did not fully return to the world of the living; instead, he became the ruler of the underworld, allowing his son Horus to rule on Earth.

This temple carving shows Horus standing behind Osiris. Horus is identified by the crown of Upper and Lower Egypt he is wearing. Osiris wears the crown of Upper Egypt and holds the staffs of kingship.

Osiris's death and resurrection were associated with the rise and fall of the Nile as well as with the daily travels of Ra through the sky and the underworld. Osiris is usually portrayed, or shown, as a bearded, mummified man with green skin, holding the staffs associated with kingship.

Isis

The greatest of the goddesses, Isis was the wife of Osiris and the mother of Horus. A closely related goddess named Hathor is sometimes also identified as Horus's mother, although at other times she is shown as his wife. Hathor and Isis are so similar that they are often mistaken for one another, and since historians do not know for sure where Isis's worship began, it is possible Hathor became or influenced Isis.

Because the pharaoh was the embodiment of Horus on Earth, Isis was also seen as the pharaoh's special protector. She is often depicted, or shown, wearing a solar disk between a pair of horns, holding an infant Horus on her lap. The symbol used for her name was also associated with the symbol for the throne of Egypt itself.

Isis and Osiris were so close—as both siblings and spouses—that they were often associated with each other's realms and powers. Just as Osiris was sometimes associated with fertility, Isis was strongly associated with death. The Egyptians believed that her role as a mother meant

Shown here is a statue of Isis holding Horus on her lap.

that she took care of the dead in the afterlife. They would ask her to take special care of their deceased loved ones.

Isis was such an important goddess that she influenced other religions as well. The Greeks and Romans each controlled Egypt for a period of time, which meant that a lot of cultural exchange took place among these three countries. Isis came to be associated with Aphrodite, the Greek goddess of love and beauty. Additionally, some historians believe that when Christianity became popular in the Roman Empire, artwork of Isis holding Horus influenced artwork of Mary holding the baby Jesus.

Bes

Bes was a dwarf god who guarded people against evil spirits and misfortune. He was especially associated with children and pregnant women. One of his most important roles was keeping watch over mothers as they gave birth to make sure no evil spirits

This carving of Bes stands in the Dendera Temple complex. Images of Bes are unusual because, unlike most subjects of Egyptian art, he is always shown facing forward.

An Interrupted History

As a culture, ancient Egypt is one of the oldest in the world, predating even ancient China. Many other cultures that began around the same time, such as those of Mesopotamia and Sumer, were buried over time and uncovered by archaeologists years later. In contrast, Egypt's most striking architecture, including the pyramids and the Great Sphinx, has remained clearly visible over the centuries. However, modern Egyptian culture has changed quite a bit.

China is considered the world's oldest uninterrupted culture because its **isolation** allowed its culture to evolve naturally. The ancient Chinese kept careful records of many aspects of their culture, and today, ancient myths are still popular subjects for art and theater. In contrast, Egypt's culture has been interrupted by multiple invasions.

The ancient Egyptian civilization lasted for almost 3,000 years. Around 30 BCE, Romans began to rule Egypt. When the Roman Empire split in two in the late fourth century CE, Christianity became the official religion, and many of the other ancient Egyptian ways of life were lost. In 641 CE, Egypt was taken over by Arab Muslims, making it the Muslim country we know today. Many Muslims consider Egyptian mythology **sacrilegious** because it goes against Muslim beliefs, so ancient myths are generally not celebrated in the country today except in museums and tourist attractions.

caused problems for the mother or the baby. He was also a god of pleasure, music, and dance.

Bes was often shown with some features of a lion, such as a mane, cat ears, and a tail. His image was kept in many homes to keep evil away. Sometimes everyday objects were made with his image on them. For instance, the Egyptians believed that drinking out of cups made in the shape of Bes's head would keep the drinker safe from illness and that putting his face on their headboards would protect them while they slept.

Bes was very popular in ancient Egypt, but he was not worshipped in the same way gods such as Ra and Horus were.

The Egyptians did not build temples in his honor, and he had no origin story. In fact, experts are not entirely sure where Bes came from. Some people believe he has origins in the African kingdom of Nubia, but there is no way to know for sure. Bes was less a god and more a figure of joy and protection.

Seth

Seth, sometimes spelled "Set," was the ancient Egyptian trickster god. He was associated with chaotic and unpredictable forces such as storms, earthquakes, eclipses, foreign lands, and the

Seth is generally portrayed with square ears, a forked tail, and a curved snout. Many experts believe he is not meant to look like one specific animal.

desert. While Ra represented order, Seth represented disorder. His trickster nature made him unreliable; for example, he protected desert caravans but also caused sandstorms.

In some stories, Seth protected Ra as Ra journeyed through the land of the dead every night. While Ra was **hypnotized** by Apophis and unable to fight him off, Seth was unaffected and killed the snake to make sure Ra could rise as the sun once more. Seth also became associated with theft and evil for his role in the story of Osiris's death and resurrection.

Anubis

Before Osiris became a **prominent** god, Anubis was the god of the underworld. Afterward, Anubis became a guide who took lost souls through the underworld that Osiris ruled. Early legends said he was the son of Ra and Hathor. After Osiris overshadowed him, the legend changed, and Anubis was said to be the son of Osiris and an ancient death goddess called Nephthys.

Anubis has the head of a jackal. Egyptians may have portrayed him this way because jackals were **scavengers** that

This picture shows Anubis weighing a heart against the feather of Ma'at.

would dig up dead bodies. The belief may have been that a jackal-headed god was the best defense against real jackals. This is why Anubis's picture is often found on tombs.

Anubis's role in the underworld was to see divine justice done. He is often shown either holding or watching the scales with which the hearts of the dead were weighed against Ma'at's feather of truth. Ma'at was a goddess of truth, order, and justice in the afterlife. The Egyptians believed that a person's heart bore the record of their life. If the heart was as light as the feather, it showed that the person had led a moral life, and Anubis led the soul to Osiris. If the heart was heavier than the feather, it was fed to Ammit, the goddess of destruction. This meant that the soul would be destroyed.

Think It Through

1. Why do you think the ancient Egyptians had so many different deities?
2. Why do you think Bes was not worshipped the way other gods were?
3. Why do you think Osiris replaced Anubis as the god of the underworld?

CHAPTER TWO

Divine Rivalry

Many ancient Egyptian gods were related to each other. Like all families, they sometimes fought; however, unlike most families, their rivalries often ended in serious injury or death. The stories about their struggles generally provided background for who the gods were, what their personalities were like, and why they each controlled certain aspects of life and death.

Atum (Ra) used magic to create Shu, the god of air, and Tefnut, the goddess of moisture. Tefnut gave birth to Geb, the god of Earth, and Nut, the goddess of the sky. Ra tried to separate Geb and Nut by placing Shu between them, but they were still able to have four children together: Osiris, Isis, Seth, and Nephthys. Together, these nine deities are called the Great Ennead of Heliopolis.

Ra and Isis

This is the story of how Isis tricked Ra into telling her his secret name.

The goddess Isis was powerful, but one day she began to wonder, "Why can't I be as powerful as Ra?" By this time, Ra had grown old, and as he walked, he drooled on the ground. Isis kneaded the wet dirt, formed a cobra from it, and let it lie in the path that Ra walked each day.

The next day, Ra was bitten by the cobra, which poisoned him. He cried out and fell down, but none of the other gods were able to help him. Then, Isis came and offered to use her power to heal him—but only if he would tell her his true name. (As powerful as Ra was, he could not cure himself because the snake was made from his own spit.)

At first, Ra would not say his name, but the poison kept spreading deeper and deeper, and he could not fight it. Finally, he consented to let Isis search through his body for his secret name, and she healed him of the poison. After that, Isis was the most powerful of the goddesses and became widely known for her wisdom and magic.

◆ ◆ ◆

Although this story is short, it tells us a lot about ancient Egyptian culture. First, it explains how Egyptians viewed names. To them, people's names were the same as the people themselves. A person's name could help them or hurt them, depending on what it was. For example, it was believed that someone whose name meant "loved by Isis" would actually be favored by Isis throughout their life. Unlike mortals, Ra had a secret name that was the source of his magical power. By learning it, Isis also gained this power. This story may have been intended to help explain how Isis grew so popular in many parts of the world.

The Egyptian cobra, also called an asp, is one of the largest and most **venomous** snakes in North Africa. It features heavily in Egyptian mythology.

This myth also has a more practical aspect. Snakes were a true danger in the Egyptian desert, and this myth reminds listeners of that danger. Some written versions of this story included a spell that was meant to protect the person who said it from poison. Magic featured very heavily in Egyptian society, so this was considered practical advice for the time. If such a story were created today, the spell would likely be replaced with medical advice on treating snake bites.

Osiris's Death and Resurrection

This story is one of the best known Egyptian myths as well as one of the world's oldest known myths.

As the oldest of his siblings, Osiris was the ruler of Earth. He brought civilization to humanity, and he was considered a wise and kind ruler. Unfortunately for Osiris, Seth was very envious of his brother. Seth wanted to get rid of Osiris and take over as the ruler of Earth.

One day, Seth threw a party. He brought out a large, beautiful chest and told the guests that anyone who could perfectly fit inside it could keep the chest. One by one, the gods tried to get into the

This picture shows the *djed*, an Egyptian symbol of stability. It represents the pillar the king of Byblos used for his palace, which means it is also closely associated with Osiris.

Variations

In some versions of this story...

- Seth turns into a monster and rips Osiris apart.
- Nephthys helps Isis find the pieces of Osiris's body.
- The chest does not float to Byblos. Instead, Isis finds the chest where Seth left it, trapped in the weeds near the riverbank.
- Seth challenges Horus to a series of contests to see who will rule Earth. Although Seth tries to cheat, Horus eventually wins.

chest. However, Seth had made it to fit Osiris exactly, so they all failed. When Osiris got into the chest, Seth slammed it shut and threw it into the Nile. Trapped in the chest, Osiris died. Seth took over the rule of Earth with his sister, Nephthys, as his queen. The chest with Osiris's body inside floated down the Nile and washed up in the kingdom of Byblos. The chest became part of a cedar tree, and the king of Byblos later cut this tree down to use as a pillar for his palace—unaware that Osiris's body was inside.

Meanwhile, Isis was very upset that her husband was missing. She and Nephthys turned into falcons and flew around Egypt, asking people if they had seen Osiris. Finally, a group of children told them to look in Byblos. Isis took on a human form and got a job as a nanny in the palace. When the king found out who she really was, he promised her anything she wanted. Isis asked for the chest and took Osiris's body back to the Nile. She hid it in the weeds until she could figure out how to resurrect him. Unfortunately, Seth found the body and chopped it into 14 pieces, which he scattered around the country.

Isis found all but one of the pieces and stitched them back together. She made a body part to replace the one she could not find and used her magic to bring Osiris back to life. However, she could not keep him alive. In the time he had left on Earth, Osiris had a baby with Isis. Isis then

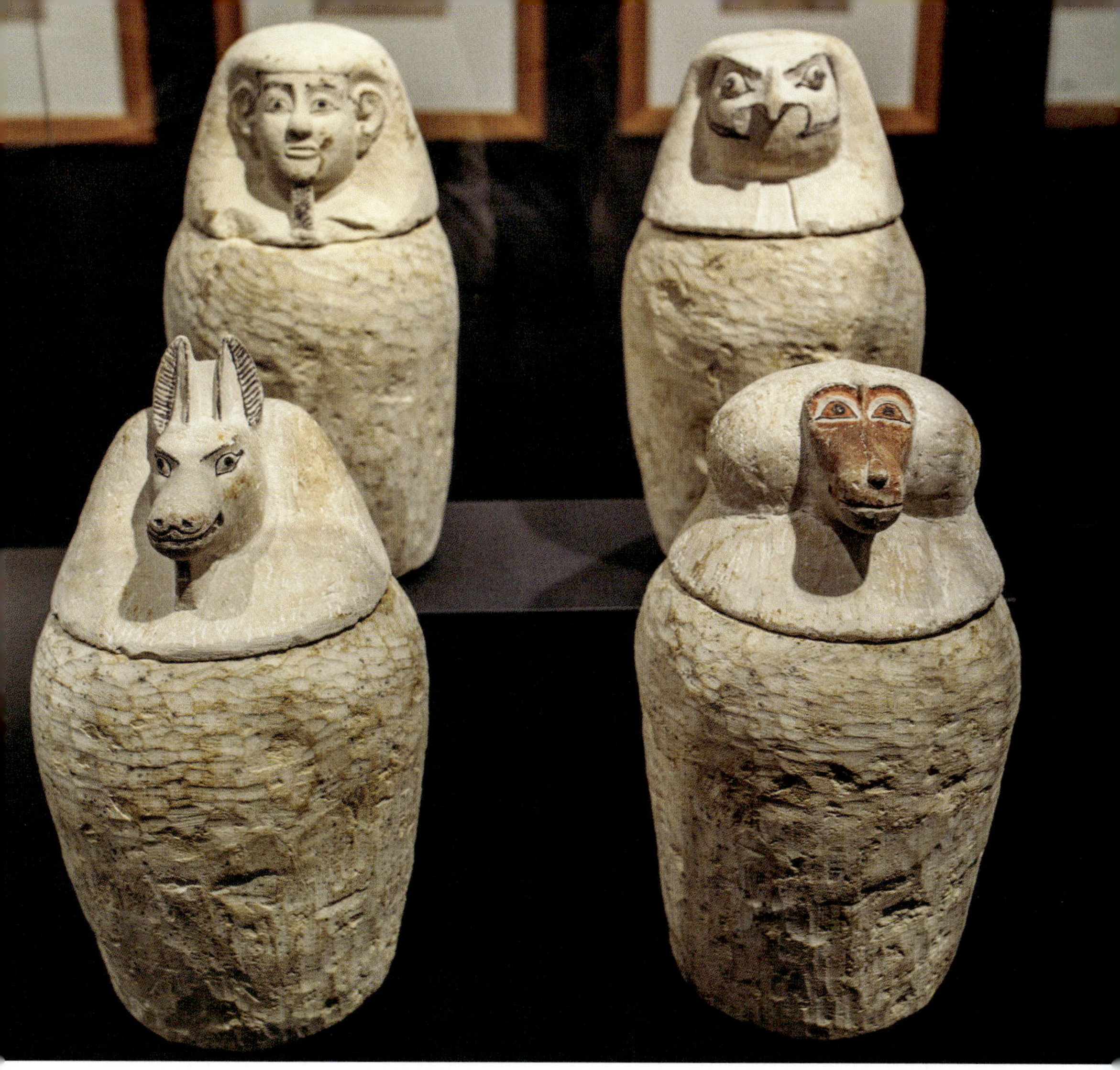

Canopic jars such as these were often carved out of stone, with the faces of gods and animals on the lids. They were used in mummification.

made sure to bury Osiris properly so he could travel to the underworld. Once he was there, he became the ruler of the dead. Isis raised their son, Horus, in secret to keep him safe from Seth. When he was an adult, Horus fought Seth and won. Horus became the pharaoh—the representation of god on Earth.

◆ ◆ ◆

This is another story that explains a lot about ancient Egyptian beliefs and customs, especially those surrounding death and

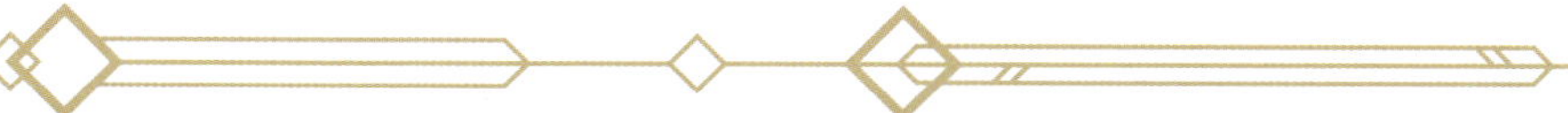

The Book of the Dead

In pop culture, the Egyptian Book of the Dead is often portrayed as a magical item that can bring the dead back to the world of the living. However, this was not how the book was used in ancient Egypt. The Book of the Dead was a collection of spells, rituals, and knowledge to help guide the dead to the afterlife. The book told people what to expect after they died, and it gave them the right spells to say to ensure that they successfully passed all the tests they would encounter.

The Egyptian afterlife could be thought of as a series of tests, and the Book of the Dead is the answer key. Deceased souls would have to answer all kinds of seemingly random questions from the gods. For example, at one point in the journey, the deceased would be asked to list all the sins they had not committed in life. At other times, the deceased would have to speak a certain spell or a certain name. The Book of the Dead told them exactly what to say. When the Book of the Dead was first **compiled**, it was only available to royalty. Opinions changed over time, and Egyptians came to believe that everyone, regardless of social status, deserved to know how to get to the afterlife.

the afterlife. The story itself illustrates the Egyptian view of the cycle of life and death. Together, Isis and Osiris complete that cycle. It also reinforces the idea that a person must be buried with the outside of their body fully intact, or whole. During the process of mummification, embalmers—the people who performed the mummification—removed the major organs and placed them in special jars known as canopic jars. Those jars needed to be placed in the tomb with the mummy. If a person was missing a body part, such as a limb, the embalmers would create a fake one for them so they could enter the afterlife with a complete body.

Another burial custom explained by this myth is the sarcophagus, or the box the mummy was placed in. Like the

Sarcophagi were expensive, so only the wealthiest Egyptians could afford them. The richer someone was, the more elaborately decorated the sarcophagus would be.

chest made especially for Osiris, sarcophagi were human-shaped and made specially for each deceased person. Many had decorations of wings on them, representing the wings of Isis in her falcon form.

—— Think It Through ——

1. What kinds of names might the Egyptians have favored for their children?
2. Why do you think Seth ripped Osiris into pieces?
3. Why do you think the Book of the Dead has been misrepresented in modern movies, TV shows, and games?

Many Egyptian myths featured the pharaohs and ideas about kingship.

CHAPTER THREE

Social Order

Many stories in Egyptian mythology illustrate the ideas ancient Egyptians had about the roles of men and women, the proper places of kings and commoners, and the importance of honoring the wishes of the gods. Along with reinforcing the culture's values, the stories are entertaining tales of adventure, romance, trickery, heroism, and wonder. They could be enjoyed by anyone, rich or poor, in a time before books, movies, video games, and other modern forms of entertainment. Stories could be told after the sun went down, with no need for light to read from a book, as well as while people worked.

The Tale of Two Brothers

This story was found written on a piece of papyrus, a kind of paper made from reeds that was commonly used in ancient Egypt. Experts believe the text was written around 1215 BCE.

There were once two brothers. The older one was named Anpu, and the younger one was named Bata. Bata lived with Anpu and Anpu's wife, and he worked for them in the fields. Bata was a very **virtuous** man.

One day, Anpu's wife made romantic advances toward Bata. He was upset that she would do this, saying to her, "I love Anpu like a father and you like a mother. Never say this again, and I will not tell anyone what you have done."

Anpu's wife then told Anpu that Bata had attacked her. Anpu sharpened his knife and waited behind the stable door, ready to attack Bata when he entered. Luckily for Bata, one of the oxen warned him that his brother was waiting for him. Bata ran, and Anpu chased him. As he ran, Bata cried out to Ra-Horakhty, asking him for help. Ra created a wide river full of crocodiles between the two brothers. With Anpu on one side and Bata on the other, Bata told his side of the story and wounded himself to prove his sincerity to his brother.

Anpu believed his brother and was beside himself with grief. Bata said, "My soul will leave my body and dwell in the highest

An acacia is a kind of tree that is native to Africa.

blossom of the acacia tree. When the tree is cut down, my soul will fall upon the ground. Find it and place it in a vessel of water, and I shall come to life again. When the hour comes, your beer will bubble and your wine will have a foul smell. I am going to live in the valley of the flowering acacia."

Then, Anpu returned home and killed his wife. Bata traveled to the valley of the acacia. He met the Great Ennead, who took pity on him and decided to give him a bride of his own. She was more beautiful than any other woman, and Bata loved her dearly. He told her all his secrets, including where his soul was kept. He also warned her not to leave the house or else the spirit of the sea would fall in love with her and carry her away. Bata told her that without his soul, he was weak, and he would not be able to save her if that happened.

One day, Bata's wife went out to walk below the acacia. As Bata had warned, the sea spirit saw her and pursued her, and she ran back home. The spirit spoke of his love for her, and the acacia tree gave him a lock of her hair, which he took and let float away to the land of Egypt. The piece of hair floated into the place where the king's washers washed their master's garments, and the hair perfumed them. The washers did not understand how the clothes had become perfumed. Finally, the chief washer discovered the lock of hair and took it to the king. The king summoned his scribes, who declared that the lock must be from a divine daughter of Ra in the land of the flowering acacia and that he should send his men to search for her.

When the king's men found her, Bata's wife decided to go with them. She then told the king the secret of Bata's soul's hiding place and asked the king to destroy the tree. The task was carried out, and Bata dropped dead. The moment this happened, Anpu's beer bubbled, and his wine had a foul smell. He ran to Bata's house and found his brother lying dead. After searching three years for Bata's soul, he found an acacia seed, dropped it in a pitcher of water, and poured it in Bata's mouth. Bata came back to life and said, "Now

I will become a sacred bull. Lead me to the king."

Anpu delivered the bull to the king and returned home. When Bata's former wife walked by, the bull said to her, "I am still alive." When she asked who he was, Bata answered with his name, and she ran away.

That night, she told the king, "I want to eat the liver of the sacred bull." The king ordered that the bull be sacrificed.

At the sacrifice, two drops of blood fell on the ground, and from them, two huge trees grew. One day, Bata's former wife walked beneath the trees and heard them whisper, "It is me, Bata. False woman, I am still alive!"

She went to the king and asked him to have the trees cut down so she could make furniture out of them. He agreed, and she went to watch the woodsmen cut them. As she stood there, a small chip of wood entered her mouth, and she swallowed it. Soon after, she gave birth to a son, whom the king named his heir, assuming the child was his. However, the child was actually Bata reborn.

The old king died, and the child grew into a man and became the king. One day, he said, "Summon before me the great men of my court, so that I may now reveal the truth concerning the queen." His unfaithful wife was brought before him and judged. Then, Anpu was summoned and chosen to be the royal heir. When Bata died after ruling for 30 years, his brother was made the new king.

In ancient Egypt, bulls were a symbol of kingship. Apis, a bull deity, may have been the very first god ever to be worshipped in ancient Egypt. Bulls were also an important part of Egyptian daily life.

◆ ◆ ◆

This myth illustrates how important divine kingship was to the Egyptians. As a commoner and a mortal, Bata was not fit to be king. However, he was favored by the Great Ennead, first by being saved from his brother by Ra, and then by being given a wife who was created by the gods. Bata's rebirth through his divine wife ultimately made him divine as well. Pharaohs sometimes appointed family members to rule as the next pharaoh, and this story shows that tradition as well.

Sekhmet and the End of Humanity

This myth features Sekhmet, a lion-headed goddess of war, disease, and destruction.

Long ago, the people of Egypt began rebelling against Ra. He was old, and they had lost respect for him. Ra summoned the Great Ennead and asked them what he should do about

Sekhmet and Hathor

Hathor is one of the oldest goddesses in Egyptian culture. She was the goddess of love and music, but when she got angry, she took the form of Sekhmet and caused destruction. Over time, the identities of the two goddesses split. Later stories say Sekhmet was created by Ra for the purpose of carrying out destruction when needed.

The Egyptians both loved and feared Sekhmet, and they often sacrificed animals at her temples to make sure she was happy. Sekhmet was known to bring diseases, but also to cure them, so she was special to doctors. When Egyptians marched into battle against enemies, they often carried banners with Sekhmet's picture on them to ensure victory. Every year, the Egyptians held a festival celebrating the time Sekhmet spared humanity. They would drink beer dyed red with pomegranate juice and spend all day enjoying themselves. The festival was also meant to stop the Nile from flooding too much. The yearly floods were important to keep the land good for farming, but too much flooding would cause destruction. Furthermore, because of the color of the **silt** in the Nile, the floodwaters looked like blood, adding another link to the myth of Sekhmet.

humanity. They suggested that he should destroy the people who were leading the rebellion, so Ra sent down Hathor in her aspect as Sekhmet.

Sekhmet fought with the rebellious humans and won, but she did not stop there. She lost herself in the pleasure of destruction and continued killing humans. The gods realized that if they did not stop her, she would destroy all of humanity, so they came up with a plan. They dyed some beer red to look like blood and spilled it in the desert. When Sekhmet found it, she drank it up and it made her very sleepy. She lay down to take a nap, and when she woke up, she was no longer in the grip of her bloodlust. She returned peacefully to the other gods as Hathor.

◆ ◆ ◆

This carving shows Sekhmet (*left*) and Hathor (*right*).

This myth has more than one moral. First, it explains the importance of worshipping the gods. The story clearly shows that if Egyptians were to stop doing this, the gods would take revenge and bring destruction upon the world. The only way to keep order was to make sure the gods were happy.

Second, this story contains a warning to the audience about losing their temper. Hathor became Sekhmet when she was angry. Sekhmet completed the job she was sent to Earth to do, but she was still angry and enjoying the destruction she was causing. This tells the listeners that losing your temper can cause you to do things you later regret.

—— Think It Through ——

1. Why did Anpu's wife tell Anpu that Bata attacked her?
2. Why do you think Bata enter the king's household as a sacred bull rather than a man?
3. Why do you think the gods stopped Sekhmet from killing all humans?

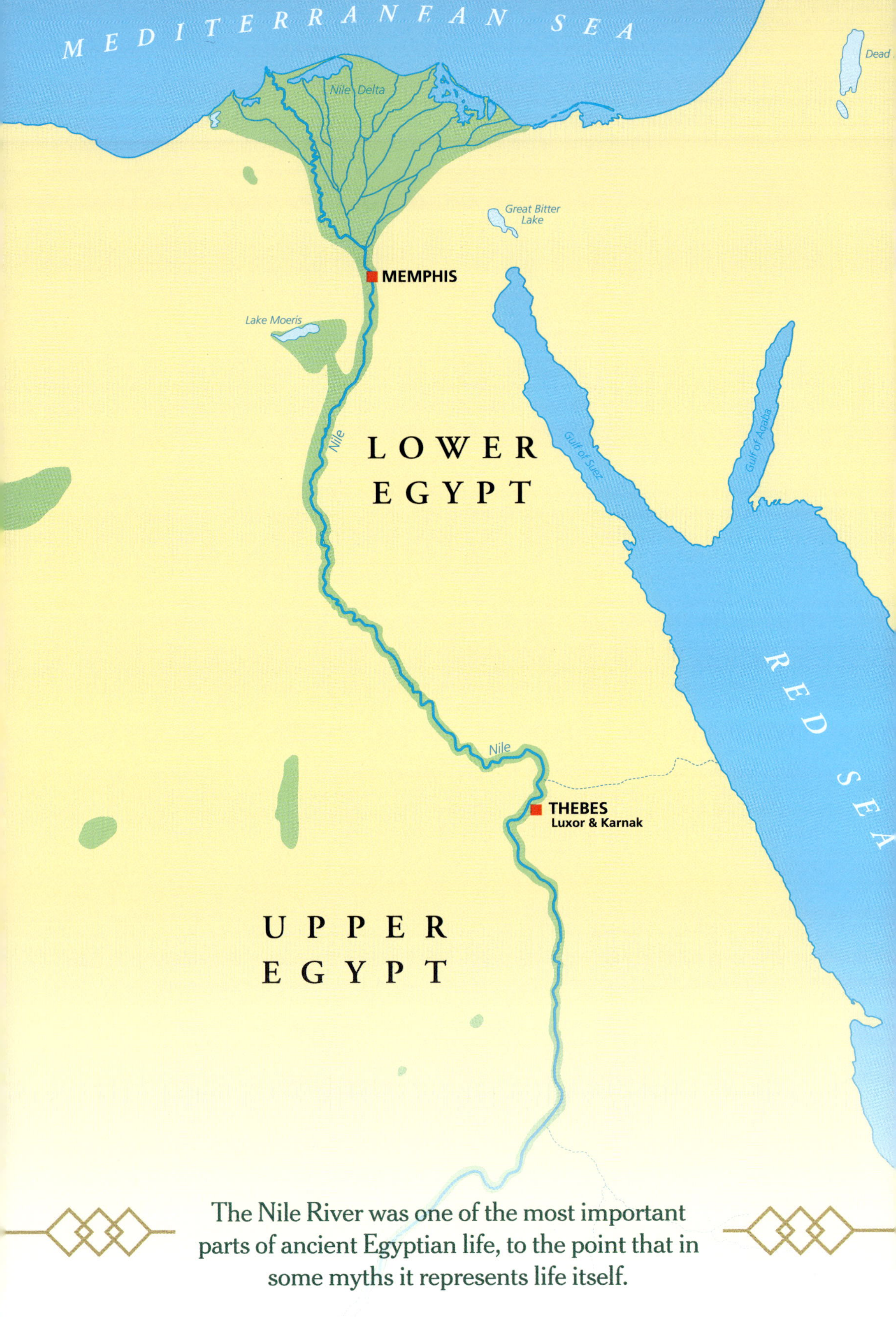

The Nile River was one of the most important parts of ancient Egyptian life, to the point that in some myths it represents life itself.

CHAPTER FOUR

The Natural World

In most world cultures, myths helped explain the world in a time when science had not advanced enough to do so. A flood or a drought, rather than being explained by weather patterns or human activity, might be explained by something angering the gods. Some myths contain a historical element; they explain a real event, but they add a mythical component, or part, to it that would have helped explain its cause to an ancient audience.

The Seven Years' Famine

This story explains how the Egyptians ended a famine that had lasted for seven years.

In the 18th year of the king Tcheser, also known as Djoser (the first king of the Third Dynasty), the whole region of the south, the Island of Elephantine, and the district of Nubia were ruled by a high official named Mater. The king sent Mater a message asking for his help because for seven years, the Nile had not flooded enough to produce good crops. Grain of every kind was in short supply, and the people had very little food to eat and were in such need that men were robbing their neighbors. Otherwise healthy people were too weak to walk because they did not have enough to eat to give them strength. Children were crying for food, and the elderly lay themselves down on the ground to die.

In this time of terrible trouble, King Tcheser asked Mater to tell him where the Nile rose and which god or goddess was controlling it. Mater made his way immediately to the king with an answer. He told the king that the Nile flood came forth from the Island of Elephantine, on which the first city that ever existed stood. The spot on the island out of which the river rose was the double cavern Qerti. This double cavern was known as the "couch of the Nile," and from this spot, the Nile god watched until the flood seasons drew near. The guardian of this flood was Khnum, and it was he who kept watch over the doors that held the waters in and who opened the doors at the proper time.

Mater next went on to describe the temple of Khnum at Elephantine and said that Khnum had not allowed the river to flood because he had not been properly worshipped. When the king heard these words, he offered sacrifices to the god and then went to the temple of Khnum to pray to him.

Finally, Khnum appeared before him and promised that the Nile would rise every year, as it had in the past, and described all the good things that would happen in Egypt when the famine

A famine is always a terrible disaster, but it would have had even worse consequences in the ancient world. Today, food can be flown to famine-stricken areas from other places, but it was much harder to transport fresh food in a time when travel often took days or months.

Khnum (*center*) was a goat-headed god of fertility and water.

ended. Khnum also complained that no one took the trouble to repair his temple, even though there was enough stone nearby to do so easily. King Tcheser immediately ordered that land near the temple should be dedicated to Khnum and that gifts should be left at the temple regularly. The king also set a tax on the people who lived on those lands; the money was to be used to maintain the temple. The original text of the decree was written upon wood, and as this was not lasting, the king ordered that a copy of it should be cut upon a stone **stela**, which should be set in a prominent place.

◆ ◆ ◆

This myth has a lot of evidence to show that it describes a real—although mythologized—historical event. The biggest piece of evidence is the existence of the Famine Stela, on which the story is written in hieroglyphs. Another piece of evidence is the fact that other ancient cultures that existed around the same time as ancient Egypt also have myths about a seven-year famine.

A story about a seven-year famine in Egypt is also recorded in the Bible. In that story, the pharaoh had a dream about seven thin cows that ate seven fat cows. He sent for a Jewish man named Joseph who had the power to interpret dreams through his connection with God. Joseph told the pharaoh that the dream

The Famine Stela was discovered in 1890.

was a warning from God: After seven years of abundance, Egypt would experience seven years of famine. Joseph advised the pharaoh to start storing up part of the food that was produced during the seven years of abundance. Thanks to Joseph's advice, Egypt was able to withstand the famine, and people from other countries traveled to Egypt to buy food because they had not been similarly forewarned. The pharaoh rewarded Joseph for his good advice. Although the Bible is not a fully accurate historical record, we know that some of the stories in it have a basis in fact, just like myths from other cultures and religions.

The Golden Lotus

This story shows that the Egyptians believed magic could be done by humans as well as gods.

One day, Pharaoh Snefru wandered through his palace. His reign had been a peaceful one; there were no wars to fight and no problems to solve for his people. Although he was happy that the kingdom was flourishing, he felt like he had nothing to do, and he was getting bored. Snefru called his chief magician, Zazamankh, and asked him to entertain him.

Zazamankh replied, "Oh, Pharaoh, life, health, strength be to you! My advice is to go sailing upon the Nile."

"I am tired of sailing upon the Nile," Snefru answered. "I have done it many times before."

"This will be no common voyage," Zazamankh assured him. "For instead of the usual strong men, your rowers will be fair maidens from the Royal House of the King's Women. As you watch them rowing and see the beautiful countryside around you, your heart will grow glad."

At this, the pharaoh became interested, and he gave his magician permission to order everything he needed. Zazamankh ordered 20 oars of ebony inlaid with gold, with blades of wood inlaid with electrum. He also chose the 20 fairest maidens in the pharaoh's household as rowers, and he ordered beautiful clothing and jewelry for them to wear as they rowed.

Everything was done as Zazamankh ordered, and soon the pharaoh and Zazamankh were seated in the Royal Boat while the maidens rowed them up and down the Nile, singing as they went. As Zazamankh had promised, Snefru was indeed happy with the journey.

Unfortunately, one of the maidens steering the boat lost the golden lotus she wore in her hair when it fell into the water. She cried out and stopped singing, which caused the maidens to stop rowing. When Snefru asked what was happening, the maiden said, "Forgive me, Pharaoh—life, health, strength be to you! I have lost the beautiful golden lotus that was pinned in my hair, and it has fallen into the

Electrum is a natural alloy, or combination, of gold and silver. Shown here is an ancient coin made of electrum.

The Lotus Blossom

Lotus blossoms are symbolic in several different cultures and religions. To the people of ancient Egypt, the lotus represented the country of Egypt. This is because the Nile looked similar to a lotus, with the delta forming the flower and the rest of the river forming the stem. Lotuses, both real and fake, were also commonly used as jewelry by Egyptians, and they often appeared in art and architecture as well. This was especially true in temples because the lotus represented rebirth. At night, the lotus closes its petals and sinks into the water. When the sun rises, it opens again.

Lotuses are also important in Buddhism and Hinduism. In Buddhism, the lotus stands for purity and faithfulness. A lotus flower puts its roots down in the muddy bottom of a body of still water, with only the flower showing above the surface. The pure flower rises above the dirty mud, seeking the light the way Buddhists seek enlightenment. Hindus see the flower as a representation of enlightenment as well, but they also see it as a sign of beauty, fertility, and abundance. Many Hindu artists have portrayed important gods sitting on lotus blossoms.

Botanists, or scientists who study plants, call this plant a water lily. The name "lotus" is heavily associated with its symbolism in myth and religion. There are many different kinds of lotuses, but the blue lotus (*shown here*) is the one most commonly seen in ancient Egyptian art.

river." The pharaoh knew that Zazamankh, with his magic, was the only one who could possibly find the lost lotus.

Zazamankh stood up and began to chant great words of power. As he did this, the waters of the river parted. The water rose up on both sides of the boat, and a small stream of water carried the boat gently to the bottom of the river. There, shining in the silt, lay the golden lotus.

With a cry of joy, the maiden who had lost it jumped over the side onto the firm ground, picked it up, and set it once more in her hair. Then, she climbed back into the Royal Boat and took up her oar again. The Royal Boat glided back up the stream of water. Then, at another word of power, the waters slid back into place, and the evening breeze rippled the still surface of the water as if nothing out of the ordinary had happened.

Snefru was filled with wonder, and he cried, "Zazamankh, you are the greatest and wisest of magicians! You have shown me wonders and delights this day, and your reward shall be all that you desire and a place next to my own in Egypt."

◆ ◆ ◆

Egyptian mythology has captivated the world for centuries. The stories feel mysterious and magical, providing entertainment while also teaching us about the culture that created them. This is, in fact, the purpose of mythology—to entertain and teach at the same time. In this way, when we study myths, we take part in an ancient tradition that links us to some of the earliest human civilizations. Themes such as family and romantic love, a search for meaning, respect for nature, balance, stability, **perseverance**, and comfort in the face of death resonate as deeply today as they did more than 5,000 years ago. Although the activities of daily life have greatly changed over the course of history, mythology shows us that humanity itself is still the same as it ever was.

—— Think It Through ——

1. Why do you think the Bible story about the seven-year famine is so different from the Egyptian myth on the same topic?
2. Why did the Egyptians associate the lotus with rebirth?
3. What do you think "The Golden Lotus" was meant to tell listeners?

GLOSSARY

appease: To make calm or quiet.

aspect: A certain way in which something appears or may be regarded.

chaos: Complete confusion.

compile: To collect into a volume or list.

exotic: Introduced from another country.

hieroglyph: A symbol used in hieroglyphic writing, which is a writing system made up mostly of pictures.

hypnotize: To put someone into a trancelike state that resembles sleep.

isolation: The state of being set apart from other people or places.

pantheon: The gods of a group of people.

perseverance: Continued effort to do or achieve something despite difficulties, failure, or opposition.

prominent: Widely and popularly known.

sacrilegious: Having or showing a lack of proper respect for a sacred person, place, or object.

scavenger: An animal that feeds on dead or decaying matter.

silt: Very small particles left as sediment from water.

stela: A usually carved or inscribed stone slab or pillar used for commemorative purposes.

venomous: Having or producing a toxic substance called venom.

virtuous: Having or showing a particular moral excellence.

FIND OUT MORE

Books

Menzies, Jean. *Egyptian Myths*. New York, NY: DK, 2022.

Moroney, Morgan E. *Gods and Goddesses of Ancient Egypt: Egyptian Mythology for Kids*. Emery, CA: Rockridge Press, 2020.

Winstone, Laura. *The Unofficial Guide to the Egyptian Afterlife*. London, UK: Cicada Books, 2022.

Websites

BrainPOP: Egyptian Pharaohs
*www.brainpop.com/socialstudies/
ancientcultures/egyptianpharaohs*
Watch a movie, play games, and take
a quiz to test your knowledge of
Egyptian pharaohs.

***National Geographic Kids*: Ancient Egypt**
*kids.nationalgeographic.com/history/
article/ancient-egypt*
Read about the history of this
amazing culture.

**YouTube: The Book of the Dead May Not
Be What You Think It Is**
*www.youtube.com/
watch?v=sHO5Z5jGM14*
Learn more about the Book of the Dead
and Egyptian beliefs about death in this
short video.

INDEX

A

afterlife, 6, 12, 17, 24
Anubis, 16, 17, 30

B

beer, 29, 32
Bes, 13, 14, 17
burial, 5, 6, 7, 14, 23, 24

C

Christianity, 7, 13, 14, 37, 38, 41

D

death, 5, 6, 11, 12, 15, 16, 17, 19, 21, 23, 24, 25, 29, 41

F

falcons, 10, 22, 25
famine, 35, 36, 37, 38, 41
fertility, 4, 11, 12, 37, 40
flooding, 32, 35, 36

G

Great Ennead, 19, 29, 31

H

Hathor, 12, 13, 16, 32, 33
hieroglyphs, 6, 7, 37
Horus, 10, 11, 12, 13, 14, 22, 23

I

Isis, 11, 12, 13, 19, 20, 22, 23, 24, 25

K

Khnum, 36, 37

L

lotus, 38, 39, 40, 41

M

Ma'at, 16, 17
magic, 19, 20, 21, 22, 24, 38, 39, 40, 41
mummification, 6, 11, 24
Muslim, 14

N

Nile, 4, 11, 22, 32, 34, 35, 36, 39, 40, 41

O

Osiris, 11, 12, 16, 17, 19, 21, 22, 23, 24, 25

P

pharaohs, 5, 7, 10, 11, 12, 23, 26, 31, 37, 38, 39, 40

R

Ra, 9, 10, 11, 14, 15, 16, 19, 20, 28, 29, 31, 32
  Amun-Ra, 9, 10
  Atum, 10, 19
  Ra-Horakhty, 10, 28

S

Sekhmet, 31, 32, 33
Seth, 15, 16, 21, 22, 23, 25
sun, 9, 10, 16, 27, 40

T

temples, 4, 5, 8, 11, 13, 14, 32, 36, 37, 40
tombs, 4, 5, 6, 7, 16, 24
Tutankhamun, 5

U

underworld, 9, 10, 11, 16, 17, 23

V

values, 27

ABOUT THE AUTHOR

Sophie Washburne has been a freelance writer and editor of young adult and adult books for more than 10 years. She travels extensively with her husband, Alan. When they are not traveling, they live in Wales with their cat, Zoe. Sophie enjoys doing crafts and cooking when she has spare time.